L & R's ALPHABET COLORING BOOK

Robert P. Helwig

Llumina Kids

Title of Work: Auto Body Characters and Parts Children's Books 1 through 4

Year of Completion: 2016

Author: Robert P. Helwig

Author Created: Entire Text

Certification:

Name: Robert P. Helwig

Date: April 06, 2017

Registration Number: TXu 2-080-413

Effective Date of Registration: April 17, 2017

ISBN: 978-1-62550-558-3

Dedication

First and foremost. I want to dedicate this book to my Lord and Savior Jesus Christ. If it wasn't for His unique craftsmanship within myself; these words, sentences, paragraphs, and characters never would've found their way from my mind to the pages.

Secondly, to my Creative Writing Instructor, James Celletti. It was him that challenged me with the ideas for the book. And to complete it.

Third and certainly not last, to you the readers! Ultimately it's for you that this book exists . . .

Acknowledgments

There are so many people I owe thanks too, for bringing this book into fruition. My parents Richard and Barbara Helwig, for giving me financial backing and support; my Aunt Linda Ehgartner, who happens to be my Agent and the person that typed all my manuscripts for me; Deborah Greenspan, for helping with all the books editing, page layouts, and publishing; Shari Reimann, for working with me on the interior layout of the books; Steve Ensign, for drawing and creating all the characters and picture scenes; my other Aunt Linda Sobieraj, members of my creative writing class, and others who weren't but still gave me valuable feedback throughout all the different drafts of writing. Thank You Everyone!!!

Thanks also to those who I unfortunately didn't mention above. You've all been a huge help during this journey.

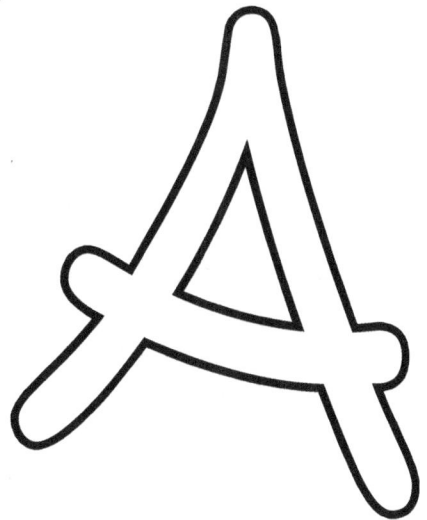

Alex the Axle

Betty the Battery

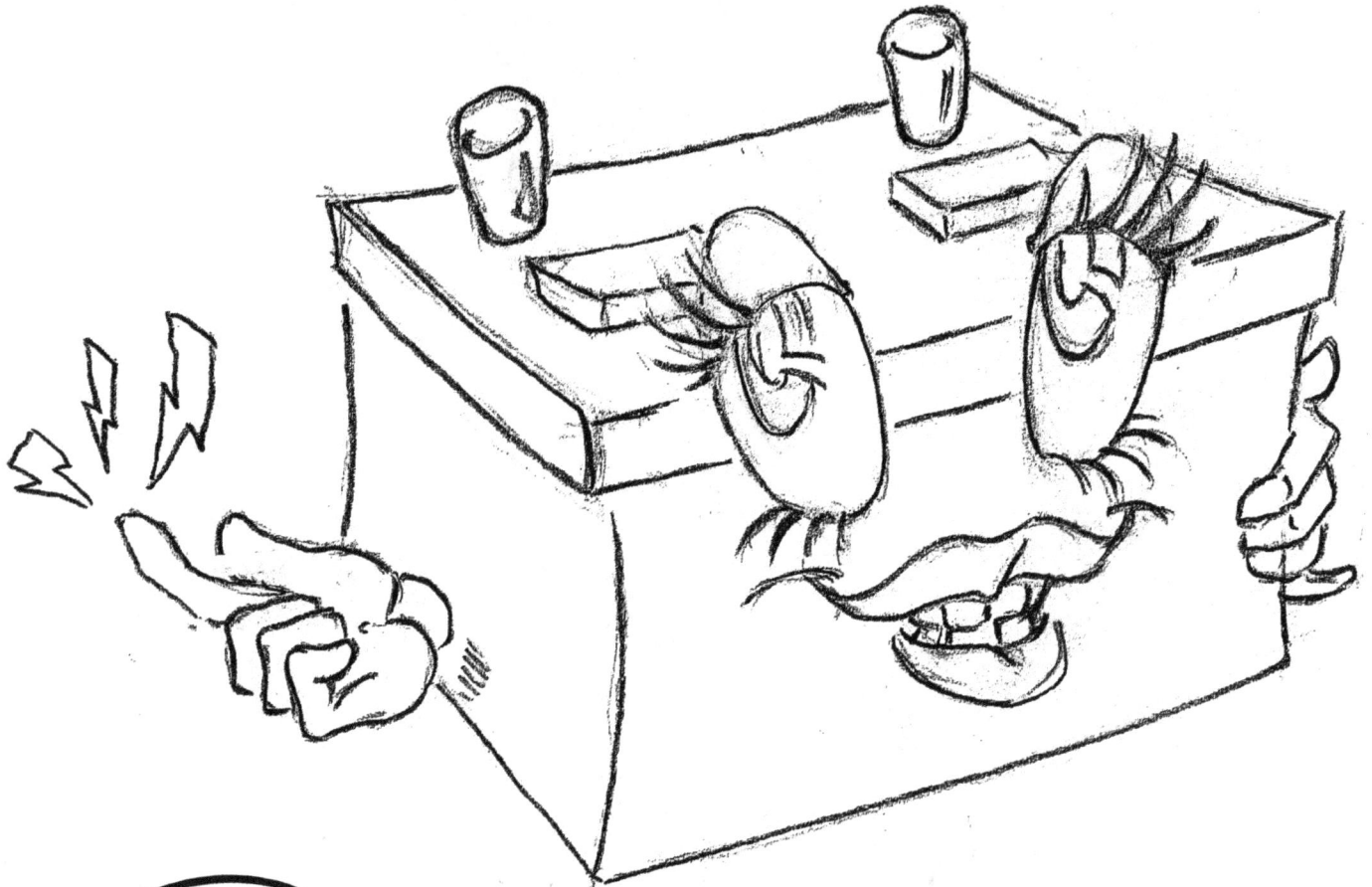

B

C

CLARK THE CLUTCH

D

Danny
the
Distributor

Elizabeth
the
Engine

E

F

Francisco the Frame

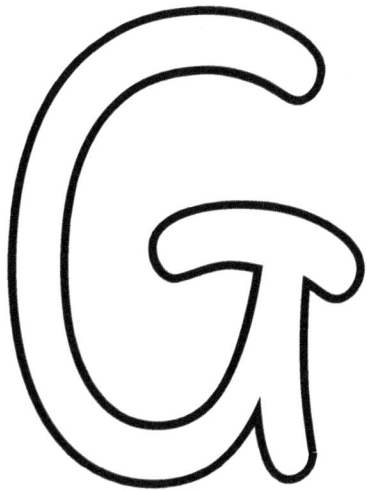

G

GREG THE GEAR

H

Harley the Horn

Ivan the Injector

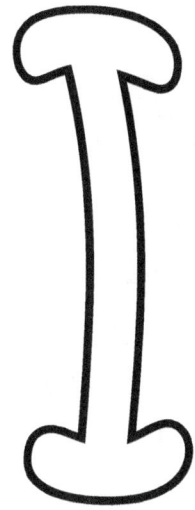

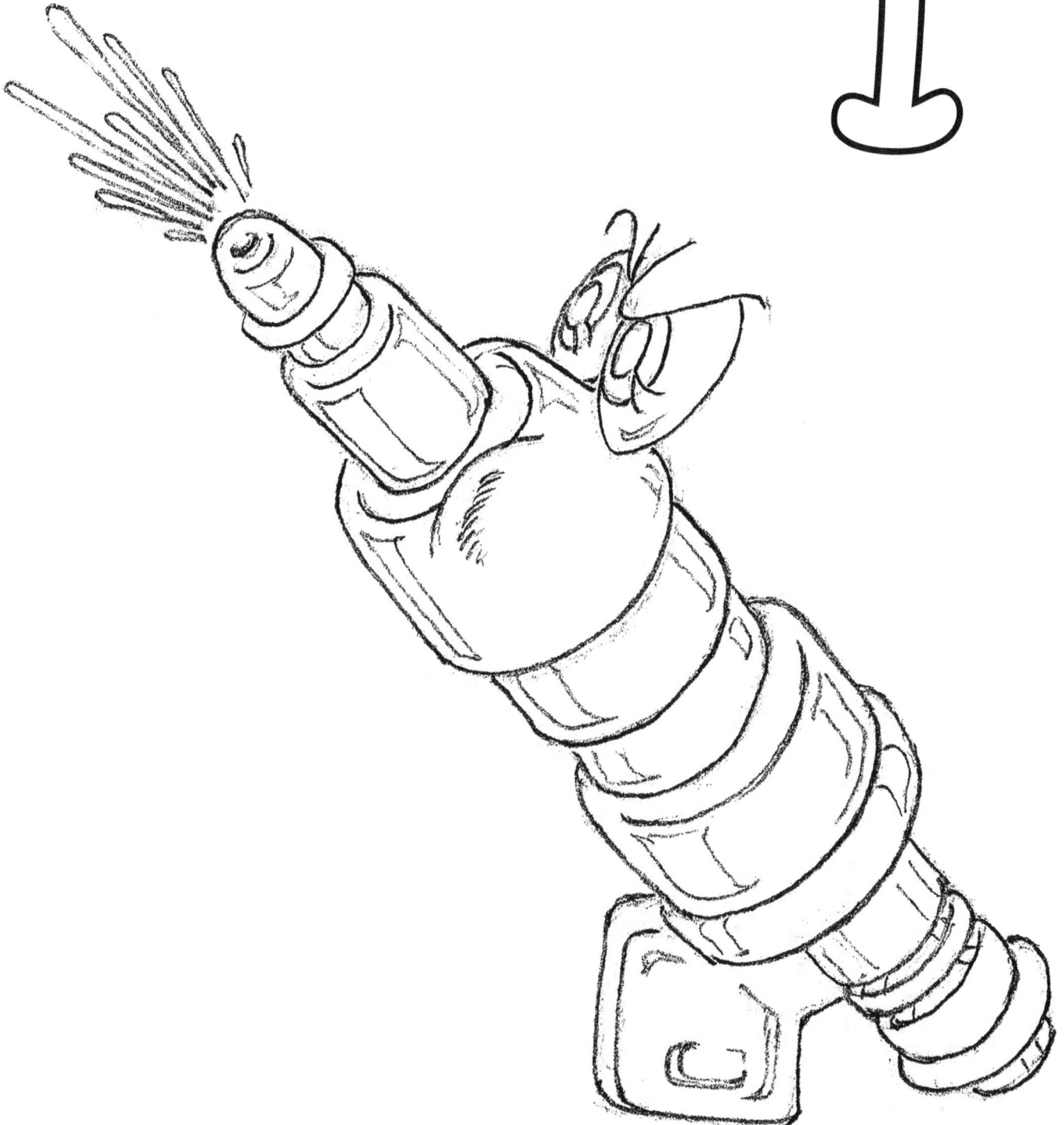

I

June the Jumper Cable

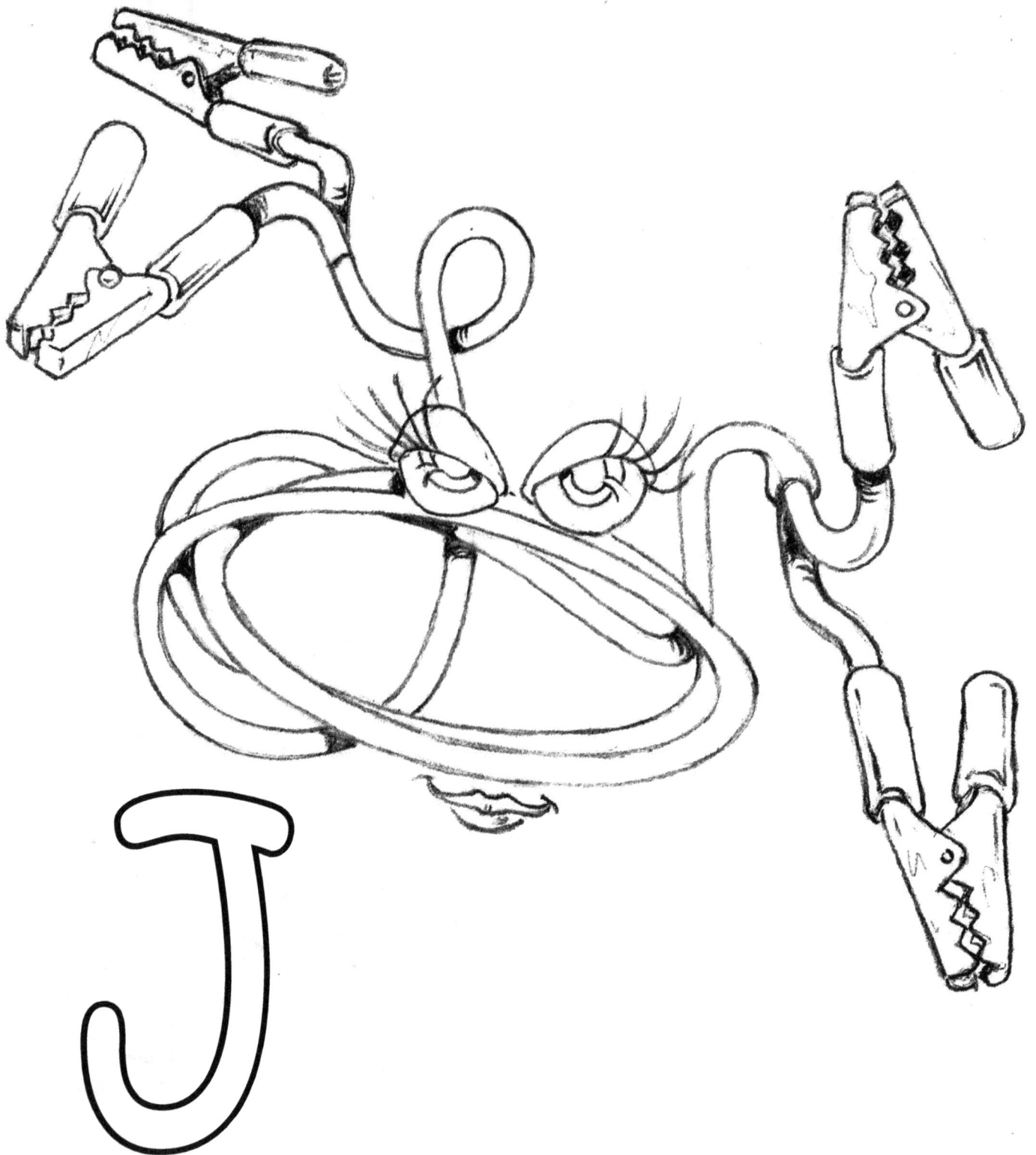

J

Kai

the

Key

K

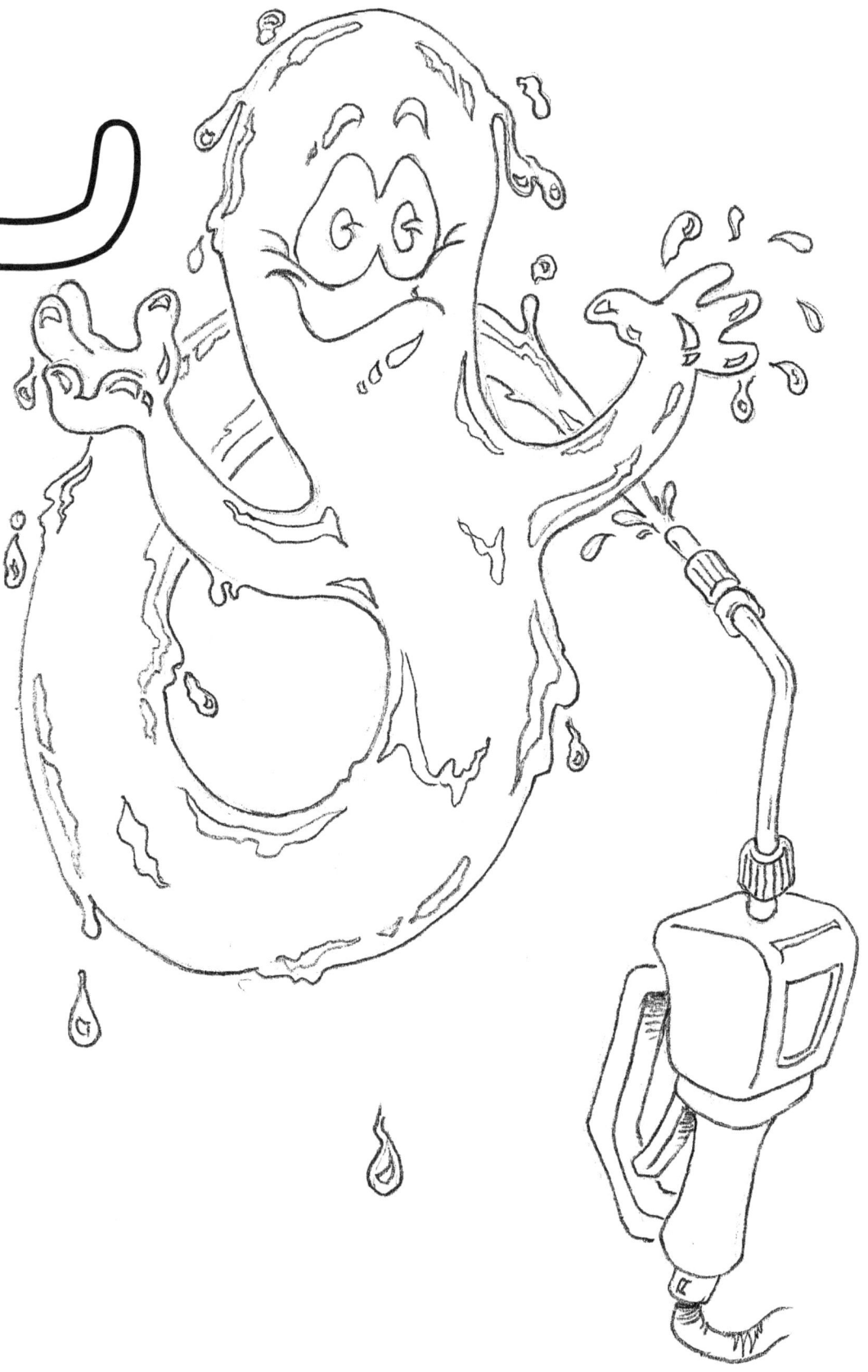

L

LOUIE THE LUBRICANT

M

Marvin the Muffler

N Natalie the
Negative Terminal

Oscar the Oxygen Sensor

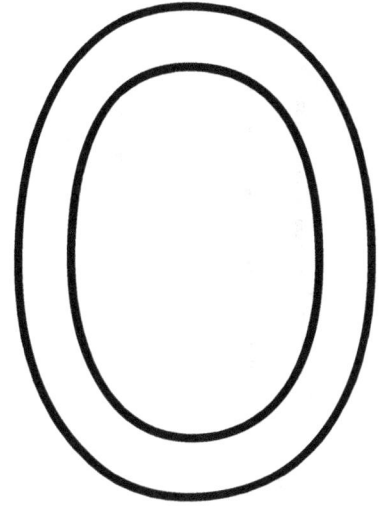

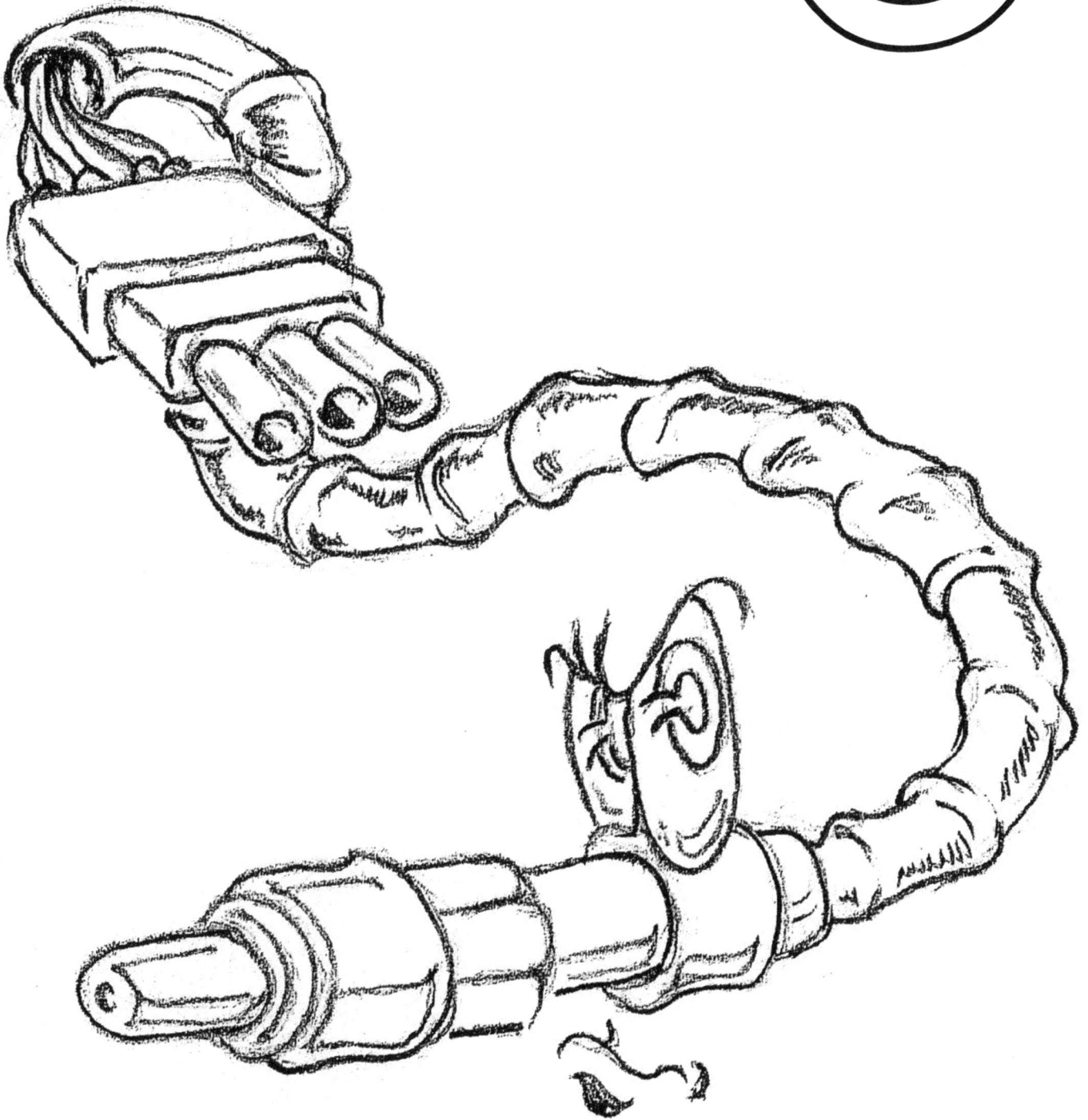

O

P

Peter the Piston

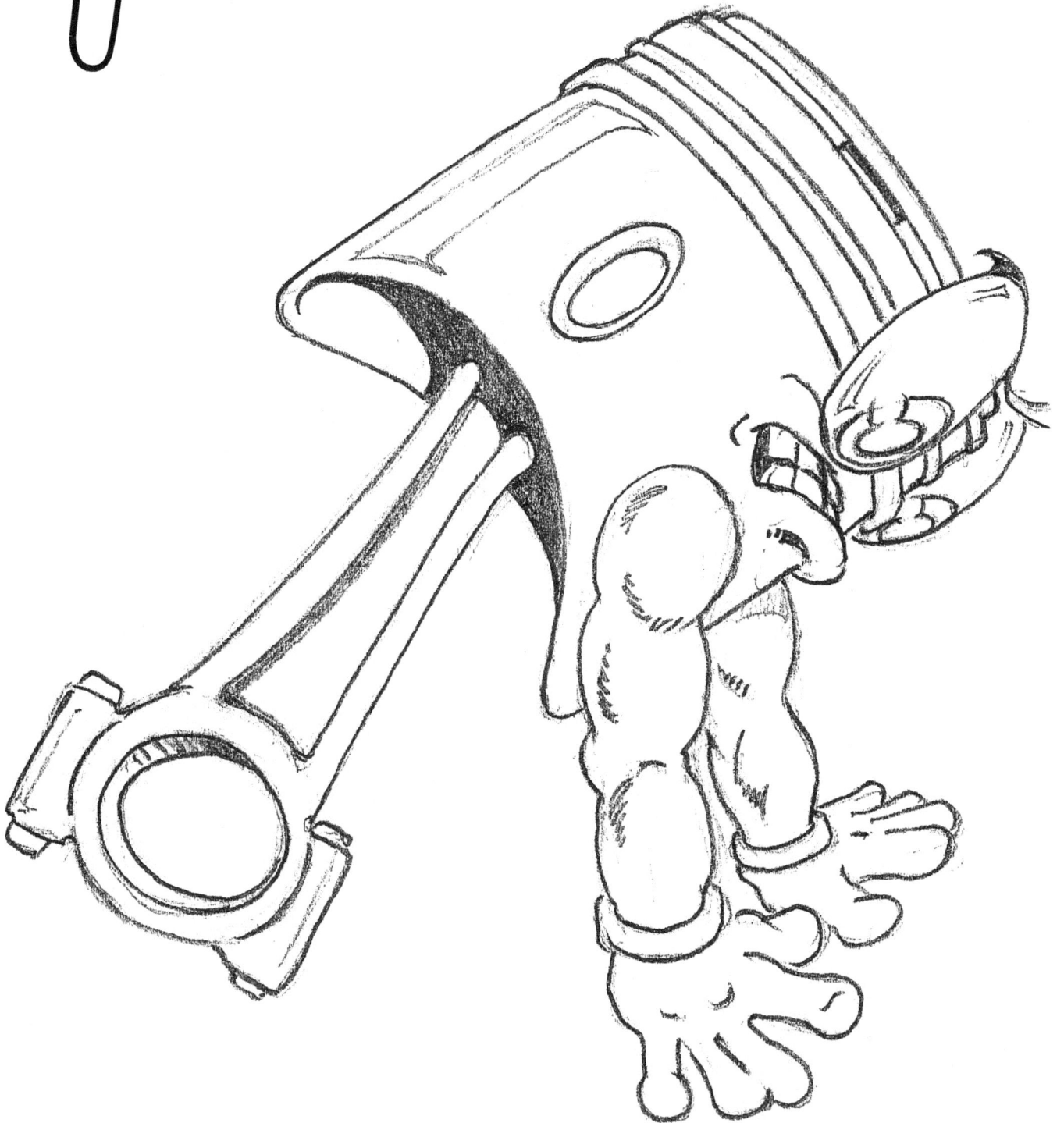

Quentin the Quick-shifter

RYAN THE RADIATOR

Sherman
the Shock Absorber

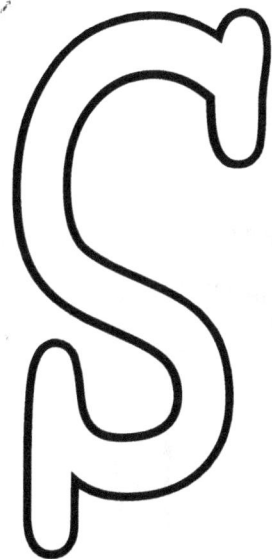

S

T

Tanya
the Thermostat

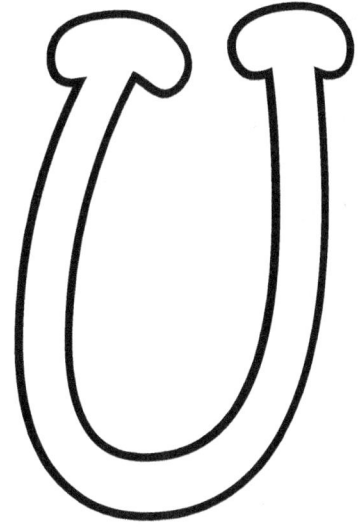

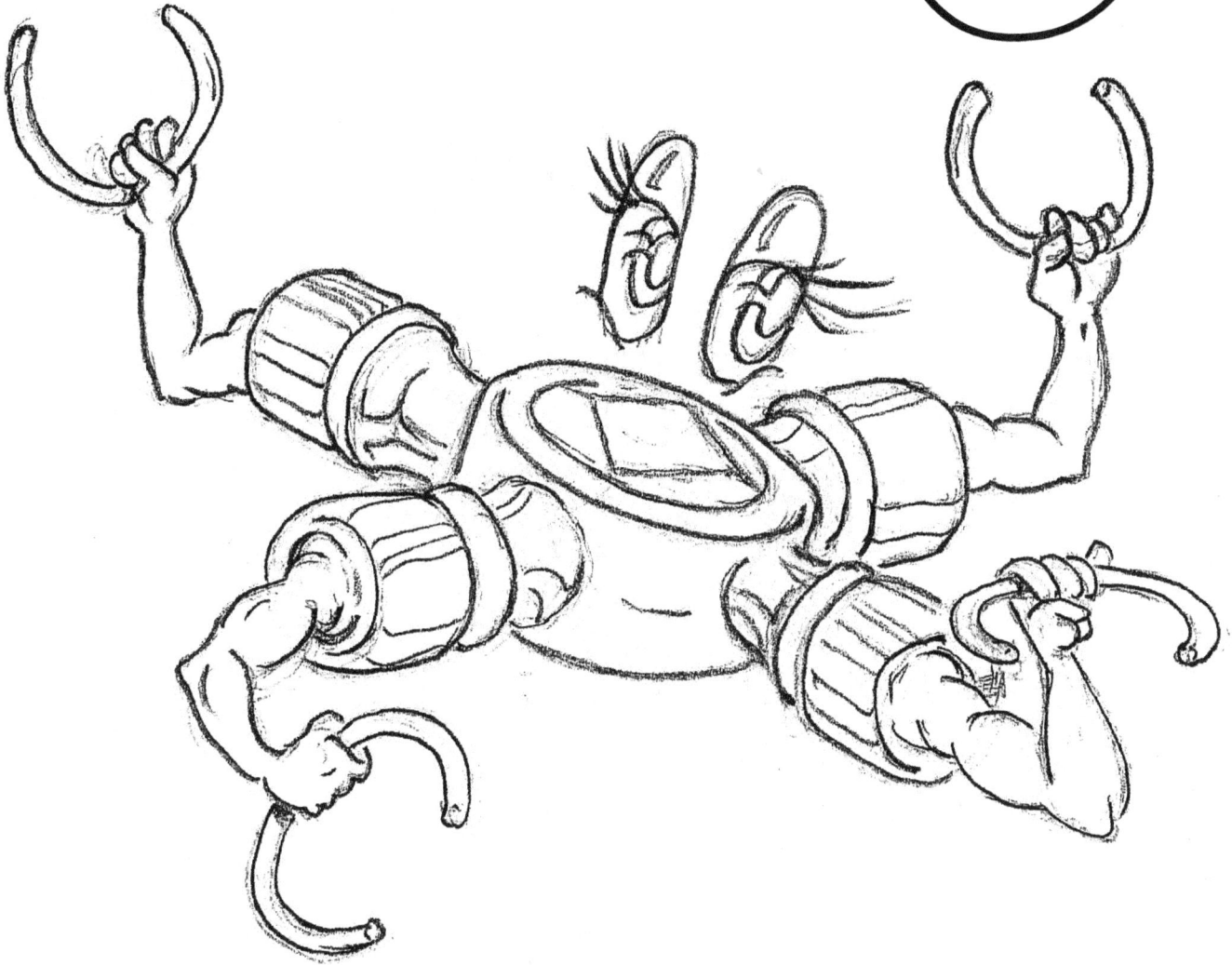

Uma
the Universal Joint

V

VALERIE THE VALVE

Willy the Wheel

Xavier the X-Pipe

Y

Yvonne
the Yoke

Z

Zeke
the Zerk Fitting

www.ingramcontent.com/pod-product-compliance
Lightning Source LLC
Chambersburg PA
CBHW080536030426
42337CB00023B/4758